queer monologues

stories of lbgt youth

Library and Archives Canada Cataloguing in Publication

Queer monologues : stories of LBGT youth /
For the Love of Learning.

ISBN 978-1-55081-458-3 (pbk.)

1. Gay youth--Newfoundland and Labrador--Biography.
2. Gay youth--Newfoundland and Labrador--Social conditions.
3. Gays' writings, Canadian (English)--Newfoundland and Labrador.
4. Youths' writings, Canadian (English)--Newfoundland and
Labrador. I. For the Love of Learning (Organization), author

HQ76.3.C32N49 2013   306.76092'2718
C2013-905954-7

Design: Vanety Fabrick, granitestudios.ca
Edited by: Sandy Newton

CONTENTS

FOREWORD

T hings are improving for lesbian, bisexual, gay and transgendered (LBGT) people these days. Public approval of same-sex marriage heralds the dawn of a new, open and sane society. On a personal and local level, however, life for LBGT youth especially can still be cruel, and even fatal. The needless pain and anguish the writers of these stories were forced to endure because they identified as gay and not straight is heartbreaking; it fills me with anger today as it did when I was young. I suffered a great deal of unnecessary emotional pain in my teenage years and early 20s and wished there had been a sensible adult around to tell me that it did not matter whom you loved as long as you loved and did not hate—and that life can be as wonderful and exciting for a homosexual as for anyone else. But there were no sensible adults around then. At least, I did not encounter them. So the story of Amy Anthony's remarkable grandmother touched me deeply. Here, in a simple rural community, was a sensible woman with a deep respect for the value of each person and a great and simple love for her grandchild that was unspoiled by conventional bigotry.

These *Queer Monologues* are moving, funny and enlightening accounts from the lives of some inspiring young people. These are all profound love stories, accounts not only of lovers but of grandparents, brothers, friends and of oneself. And since we live in a predominantly Christian society, where so-called Christian values can oppress LBGT youth, it is important to know that Jesus was not homophobic and that he would be standing with these young writers **against their** oppressors. I know many youth like Jake **Cutler, who** sought answers in the Bible. In fact, the Bible doesn't really care a lot about who has sex with whom. Prostitutes, slave girls, daughters and fathers, fathers-in-law and daughters-in-law—all are acceptable in certain circumstances. The Book of Leviticus, which condemns men lying with other men, condemns the eating of shrimp and lobster with equal force. Jesus himself contradicted the Book of Leviticus at least three times. The entire mission and message of Jesus was love. If you truly love your fellow man you will not need the Ten Commandments, or the rules of Leviticus, because if you behave with love you will naturally obey the law. And if you treat others as you wish to be treated yourself you cannot possibly be homophobic or bigoted.

The movement of history is towards a greater and more universal understanding of human rights, including women's rights, children's rights, LBGT rights, as well as the rights of other species and the environment. These rights have always existed. We just haven't always recognized them. We are moving towards more basic values and away from circumstantial distinctions and the tyranny of the majority.

It always made me angry that the straight world was in a position to accept and tolerate me or not. I could not accept that. Therefore I rejected the straight world. That was a strategic error. It's my world too, after all. It is one world and the courageous young writers who have so generously shared their stories with us here have refused to give up on that old world. They have suffered in it and for it and claim it as their own, which it truly is.

Greg Malone

PREFACE

In the fall of 1993, I attempted suicide. Afterwards, I was hospitalized in order to help me recover from the physical effects of the drug overdose. I came from an upper middle class family, was well liked at school, got good grades and was involved in many extracurricular activities, so those who knew me were shocked by what I tried to do. The reason I wanted to take my own life? I'm gay.

After I came out to myself and others, I realized that all of my homophobia was internalized. My family and friends, even my teachers, were supportive, but I was one of the lucky ones. This is my story. Since that time, I have travelled the country to share it with others. I have talked openly in the media, visited high schools, churches, hospitals, businesses and community organizations. Despite death threats, damage to my property and public humiliation that included being spit on, the overall result was positive.

Years later, when I became Executive Director of For the Love of Learning, I wanted to create a project specifically for lesbian, bisexual, gay and transgendered (LBGT) youth. While it is true that things are improving for the LBGT community, statistics show that queer youth are at a higher risk of suicide, addiction and homelessness than heterosexual youth. I found that writing was very therapeutic, when I was coming to terms with my own sexuality, and speaking to a group of people about my experiences was empowering. Given the success of the *Vagina Monologues*, I thought a show like this would be a hit.

And it was. *Queer Monologues: Stories of LBGT Youth* opened the second annual St. John's Queer Theatre Festival on July 19th, 2013, to a full house in the Barbara Barrett Theatre (Arts & Culture Centre). The audience laughed, cried, cheered, and as the last monologue finished, jumped out of their seats, and applauded the participants.

It was essential to provide queer youth from St. John's a safe, inclusive space to experience validation, growth, and healing. By sharing feelings and negative experiences through a monologue, participants and audience members created an experience that promoted acceptance and equality for all.

Times have indeed changed. Today there are support groups in St. John's for LBGT youth and their families. There is an active Pride organization and a Queer choir. There is even an openly gay Member in the House of Assembly. However, negative attitudes and stereotypes remain. Queer youth are still resorting to drugs and alcohol as an escape—and some still look to suicide as a way out—because they are being bullied at school. Their stories need to be told. And there is still work to be done.

Gemma Hickey

ACKNOWLEDGEMENTS

In 2006, an organization burst onto the St. John's scene and swiftly gained a steady footing alongside its community partners. For the Love of Learning (FTLOL) is today recognized within Newfoundland and Labrador as a dynamic arts-based charity for young people working to successfully overcome social and economic barriers. *Queer Monologues: Stories of LBGT Youth* is one of many projects that FTLOL has produced.

The success of any project depends largely on the support of many people. FTLOL would like to express gratitude to those who have been instrumental in the successful completion of *The Queer Monologues*.

Our greatest appreciation goes to Thrive (Community Youth Network St. John's) and the Government of Newfoundland and Labrador for funding the initiative.

We gratefully acknowledge the enthusiastic support of Aiden Flynn and the St. John's Arts & Culture Centre; Jenn Brown and the St. John's Queer Theatre Festival; Rebecca Rose and Breakwater Books; Helen Kennedy and Egale Canada; Cherie MacLeod and PFLAG Canada; Costa Kasimos and Planned Parenthood (Newfoundland and Labrador Sexual Health Centre); and Alice Hietala and Spectrum Choir.

Special thanks also go to Katy Warren, who performed Nathan Downey's monologue (*Jackpot*) as if it were her own;

Natalia Hennelly, for being a stellar director; Crystal Parsons, who went above and beyond her role as stage manager; Greg Malone, for his honesty; Sandy Newton, for her attention to detail; Vanety Fabrick, for her designs; Greg Knott, for his photography; Colin Doucette, for his research; Nicole Rousseau, for her advice; and to Agnes Walsh and Robert Chafe for their support.

And finally, FTLOL would like to thank the participants for their courage and dedication.

queer
monologues
stories of
lbgt youth

MONOLOGUE 1

It Gets Better

Robyn Noseworthy

Black at top. On stage a table and chair.

Lights come up on Robyn sitting on top of the table.

Before Robyn speaks, a spot of light appears Stage Right.

Can she hear my heart beat? It feels like it's going to leap out of my chest! Don't look at her too long, she may notice and it will become real. Oh, but she's so perfect. I can't help but stare. Her voice resonates in my ears long after she speaks. The scent of her perfume stays with me even when she's long gone. I watch her closely, hoping she doesn't see me. The way she moves. How her hair bounces over her shoulders with each step. Left right left right . . . stop . . . this is wrong! Look at Sean, or Joey, but not her. There's too much to risk if she finds out.

I'm being pulled into the unknown. It feels like I'm being lifted up by a tornado and thrust into a deeper part of myself. I'm afraid to turn on the light in this closet I'm hiding in. I'm smart. I get good grades. I work three jobs to help my family and save for university. I don't do drugs. I'm athletic. But none of that matters when fear is your only friend. My high school is a prison and I'm always on guard. Every day I go into solitary confinement. I long to feel the same freedom everyone else feels, but no one would understand in this small town. The way I feel about her will turn me into an outcast. Who can I tell? Word gets around.

Now she's walking toward me. I try to look at the floor but I'm drawn like a firefly to the light in her smile. She's on her way to see Mike, her boyfriend, who just happens to be the captain of the basketball team. He taunts me on the bus because of the way my pants hang. So what if I don't wear makeup. I don't want to be summed up by a stereotype. I am the way that I am, even if I don't know how to be *me* just yet.

But "wait," they say. I hear it on the television, YouTube, the radio. "It gets better," they say. These politicians and actors . . . what do they know? Nobody really knows. How am I supposed to wait when I can barely get through the next few minutes? I often wonder why the world has turned into two camps. One blind yet full of colour and hope, while the other—the one I live in—full of shadows. I'm expected to live within the shadows and never step into the light, but I really want to shine.

She's the reason I feel love. While I live in the shadows of her world I can't help but hope that, one of these days, I'll find my way out. She'll never know exactly how I feel about her, but every day that I come to this school is another day closer to leaving it. It may not be safe to tell her, to let anyone know right now, but I'll see another girl someday and my heart will beat just as loudly. And maybe, just maybe, I'll go for it.

Robyn exits.

MONOLOGUE 2

First Love

Paul Fitzgerald

Paul enters, sits Centre Stage.

When you officially "come out" it can be an enlightening experience in many ways. At least, it was for me. When I finally confessed that I was gay, the shame, guilt and pain that I felt for so long immediately lifted. Some scars remain, and they'll follow me until the day I die. They come from a time when being gay, for me, felt like a dirty little secret.

There are a lot of songs out there about "puppy love" and how beautiful it is. And you know what? It is beautiful. Whoever wrote those songs was right. But you never hear any songs about the love between two boys, do you? So when I fell in love for the first time, I couldn't relate to the songs on the radio. Falling in love was the most wonderful, painful and confusing experience in my life. I never knew any gay people and I didn't really know what gay was. I grew up in a Roman Catholic family so, as you can imagine, sex education was something I had to figure out for myself. In movies, I only ever saw a man and a woman engaged in a kiss. That's why my feelings for Kyle were so confusing.

I was 14 when we first met. As soon as I laid eyes on him I was hooked! Within three days he called me his best friend and, after so many years of feeling alone, I finally remembered what it was like to have a friend. When I started to feel those butterflies whenever he was near, I honestly thought it just meant that I truly loved my best friend. And why would I think anything of it? All boys wrestle, right? When I think back to all those times when we would laugh and roll around together, it really makes me sad. It was a time when I still had my innocence.

We were friends for about a year when my attraction for him began to surface. This time when we wrestled, it led to me giving him a massage. Touching him felt so right . . . that is, until his mom came in and we both jumped up. Kyle's only words to me were "Umm . . . thanks for . . . THAT." My response was even better, "Anytime!" After I left I thought to myself, "This must be what they tell boys and girls our ages not to be doing." But I still held onto the fact that we were two guys so it wasn't the same. All I knew was that I felt wonderful and being close to Kyle never felt as good again because it quickly became shrouded in secrecy and doubt.

I feel like if Kyle had told me back then that he was gay and had feelings for me, I would have gladly come out of the closet and proudly introduced him as my boyfriend. But it never happened that way. When we were alone we acted like a couple. Then we would hang out with our friends and I had to act differently around him. I never quite knew where I stood and it made me feel ashamed. When Kyle told me he had a girlfriend and insisted all three of us hang out together, it broke my heart. If I didn't know I was gay before, I certainly figured it all out then. Who would want to see the one they love kissing someone else!? And to make matters worse, Kyle didn't put an end to what was going on between us. But I guess that would have required him to *admit* what was really going on.

Kyle did break up with this girlfriend, eventually, but it wasn't too long until he found a new one. We still saw one another, but our time together was always accompanied by violent outbursts from him, and this continued for a long time. As if the turmoil between Kyle and me wasn't painful enough, I started questioning my own sexuality and people were beginning to notice. My mother asked me if I was gay and I felt I had to deny it, then.

The relationship between Kyle and me ended badly. He told everyone I tried to take advantage of him, and spread rumours about me. I was never more ashamed of who I was and never felt more filthy about what I did with him. It drove me so far into the closet that I never thought I would see the light from the outside again. I accepted that I was gay, but I decided to never expose my dark secret. I hid this for many years and dodged the gay rumours and accusations.

This secrecy and shame carried over into my next relationship, when I fell even harder for someone else. That relationship turned out to be similar to the one I had with Kyle. To this day, I still question whether either of them really cared for me or if I was merely an experiment to them. The silver lining is that I am out now. I'm proud to be gay and I know that everything I felt was completely natural. The only unnatural and sinful part about it was that I had to hide the most wonderful thing that can happen to a person . . . *love*.

Paul exits.

MONOLOGUE 3

Brother's Keeper

Noah Davis-Power

Noah enters, sits Centre Stage.

If you tell a lie big enough, and keep repeating it, people will eventually come to believe it. I started to believe it, I really did. Because when you're called "fag" and "fairy" every day for as long as you can remember, you start to question yourself. Do I like girls? Do I like guys? Are these people telling me a truth and I just don't know it yet? Maybe they are. Maybe they think they can kick this idea into my head.

I knew my brother Noel was gay, so I knew other people who were gay and how they hid it. I covered his trail for years. I always had to delete the browser history because he forgot. That was the weird thing: Noel could always hide it in public—he hunted, talked politics and for some reason, which made no sense to me, had lots of girlfriends. But he was so sloppy and careless about it at home. Funny thing, though—*I* never could hide being gay because I'm *not* gay. People refused to believe me, so you can imagine what school was like for me. I hated everything about it and almost everyone in it.

I was beaten every day in junior high; kicked in the head— like I said, they really wanted me to believe I was gay—given black eyes, had my lunch money stolen, and was continually called a "fag" and its many derivatives. To hear anyone else being called these things boils my blood like you can't imagine. You know, this was bad enough, but it did get worse. Do you know how? Teachers actually watched me get dragged off to be beaten and listened to me being called a "fag." Needless to say, I was pretty angry back then, but I'm getting better—though I have been tagged as a silverback. But hey, when you go from 120 pounds to 220 pounds, your nickname changes from "fag" to "fierce."

Things have definitely changed, but every now and then, if I wear a pink shirt or am walking with one of my friends, someone tosses the line "Look at those queers." It still happens—and I see red. But what I want to leave you with is that I learned a lot from all of this. Even though I'm not gay and am comfortable saying I'm straight, I understand. I lived it. I was told I was gay every day for years and it has given me a glimpse of what gay, lesbian, bisexual and transgendered people have to put up with on a regular basis.

I'll never say I went through the same thing, but you can't get much closer. What I thought about, as I was getting beaten on the ground, is that this could happen to my brother for the same reason—because he loves someone—and that's wrong. So please, for my sake, for the world's sake, love one another.

Noah exits.

MONOLOGUE 4

Sidewalk

David Le

David enters, sits Centre Stage.

I remember looking out the car window at the grand houses near my high school when my father told us we were moving to Newfoundland. I only had one year left of school and this would mean that I couldn't graduate with my classmates. I wasn't upset, though, because I never really felt like I belonged anyway.

When we got home, I dug through the mail on the kitchen table and looked at a travel brochure of Newfoundland. I was excited at the thought of starting a new life under blue skies, sunsets and rolling hills, just like in the pictures. I wanted to escape the dust and dirt of downtown Winnipeg.

I was bullied at school through most of my childhood and spent my time wandering during recess, looking for someone to be friends with. It was hard, and when I was labelled "gay" it got even harder. The irony is, I didn't know what "gay" meant! I felt isolated and often sought approval from my peers. I hung around my bullies because being used for entertainment was better than nothing. I wasn't happy at school and I remember crying myself to sleep many nights.

One day, when I was in grade three, I broke down. I was holding the door open for everyone, those double-doors. I stood there waiting for my classmates to say "thank you" as they walked through after recess. The first student came and, instead of going through the door I held, opened the door adjacent and walked through that instead. Okay, no big deal. And then the next student did the same, and so on, and so on. And as each of my classmates walked by I looked at their eyes. I don't really remember what kind of look they gave me but I felt like crap on the sidewalk—everyone knows it's there, and everyone walks around it.

When it came to choosing the high school I would attend, I decided to go to the farthest school I could manage—far from my old school and far from everyone there. It was a school surrounded by large houses covered in vines with manicured lawns. It seemed like an entirely different place. I felt that it would give me a chance to start my life over. On the first day of classes, however, a girl next to me asked, "Are you gay?" My heart stopped. I realized I couldn't run away from it—from me. I was still the same person I was before.

When we arrived in St. John's, I marvelled at everything. It was beautiful and the air was so crisp. I felt welcomed by everything around me and I looked forward to starting my final year of school. I pretended to be "normal" for as long as I could, until I fell for my best friend who just happened to be straight.

I always wanted to confess my feelings for him but was terrified of the consequences. It was a deep friendship and I wanted every moment with him to last forever, as cheesy as that sounds. Telling him how I felt meant that all of it could end. I was anxious around him and wanted to declare my feelings for him out loud, but I couldn't. Instead, I'd flirt with him and play it off as a joke.

We were walking one evening and he asked, "Are you gay?" He was finally fed up with my jokes. Moments from my past flashed before me and I paused in the middle of the sidewalk. I thought: "The travel brochure lied. It lied to me! It's cloudy, grey and cold in Newfoundland, and it's always going to be that way." He asked me again and I snapped out of my inner theatre. This was my chance—my heart was racing and I was faced with a choice. I was fed up with running away, I was fed up with that damned question; it followed me wherever I went. Hoping that it would end, I replied, "Yes."

He was okay with everything. He told me he still considered me one of his best friends. I learned that, regardless of the past, the dust and the dirt, and the clouds and the cold, you can't run away or hide from who you are. It was from that point on, after coming out to him, I felt like I belonged . . . finally.

David exits.

MONOLOGUE 5

Bakla

Riley Palanca

Riley enters, stands Centre Stage.

In high school, I was the over-achiever. Debating society, campus paper, literary folio, performance club—you name it, I was in it. As an honour's student, I always felt secure. 17 and invincible, thinking I was omniscient about the world.

My arrogance made me give a report on the merits of gay marriage in a Jesuit-run Catholic school. I spoke about what they would call evil, the unnatural union of two men. My point was there's no logical reason to oppose it. After my 20-minute speech, my religion teacher dismissed me, saying my views were leftist propaganda and should be banned from school. As if communism and homosexuality were one-way tickets to hell.

I flunked for the first time. As I walked out of my classroom for lunch, the taunting statement "*Ay, bakla, bakla,*" surrounded me. I slouched at the cafeteria with a meagre 30 pesos, barely enough for lunch, munching on a banana, the pariah of the school.

"*Ay, bakla, bakla*"—stuck in my head. You see, I never really came out of the closet. I've known I was gay since I was 7, when I had my first crush on the Red Ranger, but I never defined myself as such until that moment. "*Bakla ako. Ako'y bakla.* I'm gay. I'm gay."

In my town, I felt like a big fish banging its tail against a bowl—until it fell from the table crashing into a billion fragments. When I picked up the pieces, I was 19 and naïve, a freshman in college, surrounded by people who spoke Marx or Ginsberg or Plath. I was home.

From a local boy force-fed that his sexuality was a disease—that being gay meant being single or being promiscuous—I became part of a wider system. Older brothers were there, those who first paved the way. They never held my hand. They never led me to the yellow brick road. Instead, they painted my nails purple. They threw a fuchsia carpet on the grass and danced around like Celtic goddesses. I learned that being gay could actually be *gay*. We threw midnight raves, we danced until dawn, we slept with men, we slept with lots of men, and then I'd go home and ace my exams the next day.

Wouldn't that have been nice? That I partied all night long, realizing that being gay is nothing more than fun? That's a lie. It wasn't often that I partied. It wasn't often fun. And while it may have been often that I slept with other men, it wasn't good.

When I mention I grew up in the Philippines, a lot of people ask me what it's like to be gay there. Mainstream Filipino society would put queer culture into a continuum: on the one hand, you have the effeminate gay men, those who romp around noontime television shows for cheap laughs, and on the other, the Westernized corporate queer who, after working nine to five, frequents gay bars nightly for a quick lay.

The Philippines is a nation torn between being colonized by the Spaniards and by the Americans. From the Spaniards we learned to be conservative, religious and devoted. From the Americans we learned to be liberal, agnostic and detached. Ripped by conflicting ideologies, we have been indoctrinated by Western dogma—that freedom is good, that liberty is good, that capitalism is good—and we edge ourselves toward that. Yet we are still shackled by the tyranny of landowners, of the Catholic cult, of the social ethics that good boys bow and good girls curtsy and everyone else is a demon in a dress—an ironic image when juxtaposed with the pre-colonial Babylon, priestesses, healers and spiritual mediums who were men in dresses.

I am a Filipino gay man and I am conflicted. As a gay man, I belong to a very specific cross-section of society whose needs and concerns revolve around the next person I sleep with. As a Filipino, I want to fight for the rights of my countrymen. I try to reconcile both by being faithful to both creeds, justifying that one can co-exist with the other, or that one is independent of the other. That I can be gay and progressive, that I can be gay and Marxist, that I can be gay and revolutionary.

Turning 21 was hard. Every day was a struggle. As I walked to work, young kids would run around me shouting "*Ay bakla bakla.*" When I'd pass by the church, the priest would slam the door in my face. I'd start to perspire as I walked, as my rich colleagues drove past me. I was asked stupid questions at work, such as "So which washroom do you use?" or "Do you want to have children?" or "How do you feel about your soul?" When there was time, I would hook up—and sometimes that was fun—but other times I was taken advantage of, and in abusive relationships. When I closed my eyes I would slowly chant, **"22 and hopeful. 22 and hopeful."**

It's difficult being a Filipino in Newfoundland. Now that I have two homes, it is different. On the plus side, I'm exotic and you know it. On the downside, I feel lost, a traitor, enjoying your civil liberties while my *bakla* brothers continue to be murdered and abused. We have no anti-discrimination law. We have no equal rights law. And during the 2013 election, only one senatorial candidate supported gay marriage. We are considered substandard citizens by a corrupt government of a country we force ourselves to love.

I am grateful for my experiences here. I am 23 and free. I know it's not a perfect system, I know all of you still deal with discrimination, but I am thankful that I got to be part of a system that at least recognizes us as human beings. I'm not saying that gay life in the Philippines is that bad—you should see our gay bars: they're always crowded, because fun, sex and love become forms of social protest. When I return to the Philippines, I will be part of a massive change, a change that I know can happen because it happened right here.

Riley exits.

MONOLOGUE 6

Jackpot

Nathan Downey

Nathan enters, begins in Centre Stage then moves from left to right while speaking.

I'm going to begin by paraphrasing a quotation from notorious African colonizer, white supremacist and blood-diamond baron Cecil Rhodes: "To be born queer in Canada is to win first prize in the queer lottery of life." My inner cynical poet loves the multiple levels of irony in twisting Rhodes' words, and I gleefully imagine my edits echoing back through time and across oceans to disturb the century-old air in his tomb on that lonely hillside in Zimbabwe, causing a whirlwind of dust in his grave.

I was born queer in Canada and I feel like I've won first prize in the queer lottery of life. Let me list my winnings. My country is a haven of tolerance and progressiveness. My queer compatriots are free to marry whomever they choose. We are protected from hate speech and hate crimes by the rule of law. We are able to live our lives free from institutionalized hatred or prohibition. We have elected openly queer politicians to represent us in office. We are truly fortunate to live in such a place.

We don't live in Mauritania, or Iran, or Sudan, or Saudi Arabia, or Yemen, where homosexuality is punishable by death. We don't live in Uganda, where the news media is complicit in encouraging its people to lynch queer citizens, and whose parliament just this past year attempted to pass incredibly harsh anti-homosexual legislation as a Christmas gift for Ugandans. Nor do we live in the American Bible Belt, a region of the so-called Land of the Free whose evangelical churches preach fire-and-brimstone anti-gay dogma straight out of the Dark Ages.

No—happily, we live in Canada, an undisputed world leader in freedom, tolerance and respect for all citizens, regardless of our sexual or gender orientation. So that should be the end of my monologue, right? Sure sounds like my thesis is: "Hey folks, look how good we have it. Now let's wave the flag and listen to some Lady Gaga."

Except that that's sort of bullshit.

Let me relate a somewhat revealing personal anecdote. On June 9, 2011, an article by Paul Aguirre-Livingstone appeared in *The Grid*, an alternative paper based in Toronto. The article was called "Dawn of a New Gay." To summarize the infamous article very briefly, the author discussed how, for him and his peers in queer old Toronto, the fight was over.

No longer did they need to participate in Pride parades or meaningful activism. They were simply free to enjoy their lives as queer citizens however they best saw fit.

And I have to admit, I sat back and said, "Finally, someone has articulated my exact feelings on my sexuality." I, too, had emerged queer in a society where the preceding generation of activists had done all the hard work for me. I lived in this great country and in this great era that let me be exactly who I am. I had incredibly supportive parents. I had thorny armour and an acid tongue to counter the very sparing bouts of homophobia I'd experienced in my lifetime.

I remember being amazed at the instant backlash that Aguirre-Livingstone's article caused. I thought surely the legions of detractors were stuck in a bygone age, ignoring the incredible progress the queer cause had made before arriving at this august era. I was puzzled. But then I realized that the dissenters were right. The author was writing from the perspective of having been born an urban queer in a tolerant country. No doubt he was speaking for a significant number of people, and I included myself in that category. We alone were the holders of the winning ticket. Lucky us.

I gave it thought for a few days and realized the viewpoint was incredibly selfish. That was neither the first nor the last time I'm sure I'll admit to that particular personality trait.

My initial viewpoint, like that of the author of "Dawn of a New Gay," had failed to account for the 17-year-old gay kid in Grand Falls forced into the suffocation of the closet by the disapproval of his family and the poisonous doctrines of religion. It failed to account for the 25 to 40 per cent of homeless youth who identify as LGBTQ. In brief, our viewpoint failed to account for, basically, anyone on the margins. Like in the actual lottery, there are only a few winners—and what right did we have to be so smug, so unbelievably sanguine?

We had, we *have*, no right. We are the winners by virtue of our highly fortunate circumstances and not because we did anything to deserve it. Though things in our country are better all over, there are still large percentages of queer people who have lost. And the only reason things are better for everyone is because brave queer people from this and from previous generations fought against injustice and strove for equality.

I regret my initial selfishness and lack of clarity. I can only hope that Aguirre-Livingstone regrets his. As partial penance for my smugness, I am adding my voice to the chorus, to the ongoing conversation. I recognize that queer advocacy won't become moot until everyone wins—or better yet, until the proverbial lottery slips into obsolescence altogether. And while we should all hope to see that day in our lifetimes, it is not yet upon us.

Nathan exits.

MONOLOGUE 7

Letter

Jake Cutler

Jake enters, stands Centre Stage with hands in pockets.

Dear 11-year-old me,

This will be a hard year for you.

You'll start to grow hair on your legs. You'll be okay with this, but others will not. They'll give you razors and shaving cream tied up in a pretty pink bow like a sacred passage into womanhood. You won't be prepared for what comes next.

You'll start to notice your flat chest, which made you look like other boys, growing under your shirt. Your breasts will look like lumps and feel strange. You'll try everything to make them flat again. You'll wrap yourself up in plastic and duct tape. This will hurt you and make you pass out in gym class.

Your doctor will tell your parents and they'll be mad. They won't understand. You'll feel like no one really knows you or gets who you are. You'll become angry and feel lonely. You'll hurt yourself and this won't make you feel any better.

You'll notice that your hips are getting bigger. So will everyone else. Your mother will tell you that you are becoming a "lady." The boys in school will treat you differently and will make you feel like a "thing." They'll put a ruler under your skirt to lift it up and call you things like "whore" when you wear your normal clothes and "prude" when you try to cover up.

The boys you once called friends, who played with you in the mud just one year before, will avoid you except when they grab at you or catcall you. You'll try to hide by wearing your brother's baggy clothes—only to find that the attention is still on you. You'll be called things like "it," "dyke" and "shim" and this won't make you feel very good.

When you go home, you won't find sanctuary there because you'll often fight with your mother. At the mall shopping for girl's clothes, she'll point out to you that you don't have any female friends. Oh, but you'll notice girls. You won't be able keep from smiling at them in class. They'll call you "gross" and tell you you're a "freak" and you'll believe them. You'll feel very small and broken and when you get your first period your mother will throw a party. You'll cry every day. You'll read your Bible to try to find the answers, but won't find any there.

Dear 11-year-old me,
   The world will be hard, like swimming in a cold sea, the salt burning your lungs as you try to keep your head above water. This will continue for another couple of years until you give in to the world. You'll put on a dress and a wear a mask of makeup covering up the boy you wish to be. This will make you friends and your life will get easier until one day (you'll know when this is because it will seem like a weight has been lifted from your shoulders) you'll feel like you can fly.

This will be a day in your future where you'll find your answer. It'll come to you just as you're being punched in the face at a bar in your hometown. You'll pick yourself up from the floor, wipe the blood from your mouth and the words will come so naturally. as if God put them in there, hiding under your tongue all this time.

"My name is Jake and I am a man."

Jake exits.

MONOLOGUE 8

The Best of the Worst

Amy Anthony

Amy enters, stands Centre Stage.

If you had to pick the best and worst days of your life so far, what would they be? It seems like such an easy question, right? You fail an exam; you pass your driving test; you have an amazing date; you get dumped; you have a car accident; you find 50 bucks on the street . . . how can you possibly single out one day of your life when so many things happen every day? I knew, after some thought, that I had in fact experienced both in one day.

It was July 9, 2011—the day I saw my grandma Beu for the last time. She had been battling leukemia for four years when all of a sudden it magically disappeared from her system. I got my hopes up, of course, but not Beu. She was convinced it was her body's way of recharging itself in order to deal with what was to come. She was headstrong like that, and right.

Beu was a churchgoer. She always made me go with her, every Sunday like clockwork, when all I wanted to do was watch cartoons. I was forced into a dress, given a handful of money for collection and dragged into a pew. After it was over, we would head down to her and Bamp's house (that was my grandfather). They always had a big feed of moose, or roast, rabbit or turkey, and every salad and side you could imagine. I became a vegetarian at a very young age, so my diet at their house consisted mainly of potato, beet or mustard salad with a side of coleslaw. They tried to accommodate my early vegetarianism, my short haircut, my not having boyfriends, but they "didn't understand."

I heard that phrase—"I don't understand"—all my life.
I realized early on that I was gay. When most girls my age
watched movies, wanting so desperately to be like the girls
they saw, I just thought they were cute and wanted to date
them. I wasn't comfortable coming out in high school because
there were no "out" gay kids there. From what I could tell,
there were only a handful of us anyway; I know this because
we all hung out together and, secretly to one another, had
come out in our own way. We actually even faked straight
relationships with one another to keep some sort of facade
going for our parents' sakes. The boys definitely had it harder
than the girls, so pretending just made everyone's lives easier.

When I left for university, I decided to come out to my
parents. It wasn't met with much resistance but took time to
settle in. The only request from them was that I not tell my
grandparents. At first I agreed to it—you hear of so many
stories of people's parents reacting horribly to something
like this, so I was kind of relieved—but after a while it really
bothered me. I mean, why should I have to introduce my
girlfriend to relatives as my "roommate" or "best friend" at
family functions? This never made sense to me, so I slowly
started to tell family members and gauge their reactions.
The usual response was: "As long as you're happy and aren't
hurting anyone." Unfortunately, I waited a little too long to
tell my grandparents.

My mother called me one day and asked me to come
home as soon as possible because things weren't looking
good. My partner Sara packed my sobbing half-hysterical self
into the car and drove me six hours across the island to see
Beu. When we got to the house, Sara and I walked in to find
Beu very frail and tired. She could barely find the strength
to give me a hug but she was thrilled to meet Sara. I had
spoken often to Beu about Sara, so it was only natural that
she wanted to sit and ask her about her family and where
she worked, who she's related to and so on. It wasn't very
long before she needed a rest so I decided to come back the
following day to hang out with Beu on my own.

After a good night's sleep Beu seemed in much better spirits and wanted to sit to the table for a proper cup of tea and a biscuit. We sat for hours, talking about the past, how much she loved being a part of raising me. She had a few good cries and more laughs than anything else. She brought me into her bedroom and gave me a box with all the broaches my grandfather had made her over the years. I told her to stop giving stuff away because she wasn't going anywhere anytime soon, and that's when she told me she wouldn't be taking her medications anymore, that it was her time to go and that she was ready to be with Bamp. I fought back tears and told her to not be so foolish, but deep down I knew she had given up when he died. She always said, "The sickness is just getting me to him quicker."

When we went back to the table something unexpected happened. She started to tell me a story about my cousin Mary Ann, who just so happened to send her a care package from South Carolina. When Mary Ann was young, her mother died tragically. Her father became bitter and got married again to a very hateful woman. They both treated Mary Ann with such disrespect that she ran away from home. She lived with my grandparents for a while, then took off to the mainland and eventually found herself in the States where she met the love of her life, Emma.

Mary Ann and Emma would come back to the island every summer for weeks on end and stay with my grandparents. I had heard this story a million times, but in the same way. Beu had a motive this time. She said, "You know, Mary Ann and Emma will always be welcome in my home. They are good people. You know, me and your grandfather aren't stupid, we knew they were Lizzies. That makes no difference in this world. They are good people." My eyes immediately filled up. I got up to make more tea so she wouldn't notice, but she grabbed my hand, held it as tight as she could, and said, "Sara is lovely. She is really smart and nice and you keep good company." And with that a slew of people came in through the front door. I tried to walk away but again she didn't let go of my hand. "Be happy, that's all Nan wants."

She got up from the table and stumbled into the pantry where she brought me out a loaf of her famous banana bread she'd made the day before I got home. I loved that bread and she wouldn't give anyone the recipe. "That's the last one so keep it in the freezer and enjoy it over time." She gave me a big hug then walked over to Sara and gave her a big hug and said, "You take care of my girl now, Jennifer." I didn't hear that part. Sara waited until we got to the car to tell me that Beu got her name wrong, which made me howl with laughter.

Nan held on for another week. The days leading up to the funeral were very sad, but she had everything organized— jewellery labelled, clothes labelled—and, unknown to me (who thought she had the last of the banana bread), she'd left a deep freeze full of them! I guess we all have our secrets. I didn't have to tell Beu I was gay, she knew all this time—and most important, she understood. I keep kicking myself for the things I could have said in those last moments we shared, but Mom says not to dwell on it. I just wish I had her here to talk to instead of staring into the freezer at all that banana bread.

Amy exits.

MONOLOGUE 9

I Came Out

Erin Edwards

Erin enters, stands Centre Stage then moves from left to right while speaking.

We went everywhere, my family and me.

Growing up in rural Newfoundland has this way about it— you can leave but you always want to go back.

And so we did.

We went everywhere.

It was a sunny August Monday when I was born. Cool breeze blowing and the birds chirping outside, something welcomed me in the air that morn.

We went home.

When I was 3, can hardly remember the day, my smiling mother said, "Precious, we're moving."

With loving eyes I trusted her; Dad got a job—it was the only way.

We went to the city.

From age 3 to 6, I did as all toddlers do.

Went to school, made new friends, ate happy meals, too.

Fell off my bike a few times and got boo-boos.

Life went on.

"Never cross the road when I'm not with you," Mom said.

And so, walking home from class, I sat on the grass across from my house, my mom lost track of time.

She came running, then held me close, I was relieved when she took my hand.

We went home.

"Sweetie, Daddy got a new job, we're moving again."

This time I cried and I cried—I didn't want to leave my friends and my school and my playground and . . . .

"It's just around the bend!" she said.

We went to Alberta.

Siblings and belongings and my stuffed bear in tow.

Started a new life in a new place: new school and new interests.

I overcame my speech impediment and wanted to join soccer, only because I liked the way the grass smelled when first mowed.

We went cleat shopping.

Mom didn't like apartment-style living, so we came home.

We drove home, actually—right across Canada.

Only border I missed was between Saskatchewan and Manitoba.

Cuddled up, microwave next to me, was really cozy, I guess, or maybe I was missing my BFFL; I was all alone.

We went home.

In grade three, I had a mind of my own—rugged explorer and soccer player.

Ice cream and Velcro sandals, one-piece swimsuits and track pants.

Passion Flakies were my passion, Backstreet Boys and Spice Girls and don't tell me that Mel C wasn't cool—I don't wanna hear from no haters!

Life went on.

Influential teachers taught me left from right and wrong from right.

I got in trouble once for sending dirty notes (not texts) in class.

Grade seven I joined church choir and hockey—besides teachers,

Mom and television were my biggest influences, but I was still so young and bright.

I went on living.

School, 40 per cent; boyfriends, 10 per cent; sports, 50 per cent—my life in a nutshell.

Junior high was a time to learn and to grow, and figure out what the hell this vagina did to me once a month.

Sweat glands and puberty and girls started to look a whole lot better to me than usual and, well,

I went searching.

Senior high, and sometimes I felt so unbelievably low. Caught between what my body was telling me to feel and what my parents and society were telling me not to—

I didn't know if it was right, but I knew when I held her hand it felt right.

My mind was about to blow.

We went sneaking.

Sneaking out late at night, against a God I was taught to believe in, behind my parents' backs, sneaking away for bathroom breaks, two late-night lovers who were friends by day.

Away from the judgement, away from the ones who believed we had sinned.

We went to a different kind of heaven.

Pretty soon I wondered, "Am I just in this for the thrill?"

Perhaps I could ignore what I wanted and focus on other things like straight friends and straight As and straitjackets and straight up, straightness?

That was easier than breaking news to Mom and Dad and expecting them to be chill.

Life went on.

Life went on and school went on and I graduated at the top, with scholarships and awards, and money was practically thrown at me.

Hearing about exciting opportunities for this young, successful, straight woman.

My future looked so promising, and I promised myself that that small town would never find out—it would've all turned out differently.

I went and I wondered.

I went home and that night under dim light I wrote in blurred penmanship from the constant stream of tears:
"To my Mother and Father, to the people that I love the most, all I'm asking for is your acceptance, your love. This does not change who your successful hard-working daughter is."

I went to sleep.

I woke up and stowed that letter away, my feelings along with it, bottled up inside and shut the drawer tight; I'd wait for the right time.

I moved away from home, on my own, where I could be me.

And in residence I had the best lesbian sex EVER and nobody gave a shit.

Life went on.

Christmas came and I went home and still no changing my parents' conservative minds.

I could tell they were so oblivious to it and they didn't pry, so I didn't try.

The letter was in my drawer and remained there for six months more.

I went back to the city.

It was the summer after my first year at MUN. I'd had a good year, had a good run.

Was now the time? I couldn't tell but I figured, what the hell.

"I prefer girls," my email had said. I knew I'd be in bed by the time it was read.

My fingers so shaky, I needed to pee—but I had to do this if I really wanted to be me.

Listened for Dad's footsteps into the study,

heard a mild shout—and that, ladies and gents,

was the summer

I came out.

Erin exits.

MONOLOGUE 10

Pride

Joshua Jamieson

Josh enters, stands Centre Stage.

I was 15, trembling in front of my mother's bedroom door, clasping a neatly folded piece of paper in my hand. The door was open slightly and I could see her lying on her bed, scribbling in a crossword puzzle book. She heard me at the door, took one look at me and immediately knew something was up. I entered her room and reluctantly handed her the now crumpled paper. As she read it my heart was pounding.

I'd written that I was bisexual, a calculated decision on my part for two reasons. One, I could back away from relationships with men if that wasn't the way I wanted to go (but I knew the difference deep down, whether I wanted to admit it then or not). And, two, the possibility of giving my mother a grandchild wasn't completely out of the question.

After waiting for what felt like an eternity, she looked up, smiled and told me that she loved me. We didn't talk about it again until a few months later. I was heading to the mall to see a late movie with some friends. After the show, we ran into car trouble and I ended up having to stay out later than expected. When I finally arrived home, my mom was hysterical because her imagination had run wild. She wondered if I had even gone to a movie, thinking that I was on some kind of covert date. I reassured her that I *had* indeed seen a movie, and there was no secret rendezvous.

This actually triggered a deeper conversation, one that needed to happen. By this time, I knew I was gay and she did too. She confessed that she thought my life would be harder, but I told her it wasn't a choice. She agreed and told me that no matter what happened we'd get through it together. We had both done some research at this point. She had read everything there was to read on AIDS and admitted that it made her worry, but that gave me the opportunity to explain to her that there was a difference between AIDS and HIV, and that I had every intention of practising safe sex.

We stayed up all night just talking things out on the couch. That conversation closed the loop my letter had started. I was gay, out to my mom and we were ready to move forward. The next steps were slightly easier because they weren't taken alone. The circle of people who knew would only grow from that point, expanding to include friends at high school and then extended family. Mom and I made an almost unspoken arrangement, I gradually told people at school and she leaked the news into conversations with her siblings, who in turn shared it with my cousins, and so on. It seemed almost natural, and I only say "almost" because, at the time, we were in uncharted territory.

Reactions were all positive for the most part, too—I had one innocent aunt, who suggested that it might be a phase, but Mom assured her that wasn't the case. One of the best reactions I ever received was when I told a girl who sat in front of me in French class. I tapped her on the shoulder and whispered it to her one afternoon and she actually exclaimed, "WOW, that's so COOL! Now we can go shopping!" As if my sexuality suddenly made the activity permissible.

It felt great to talk openly to my family and friends about my sexuality, but at the time the only way for me to talk to other gay people was online. Sure that was all right, but I really wanted to meet people who were "like me" in person. My mom and I found a group in St. John's called NGALE—Newfoundland Gays and Lesbians for Equality. She dropped me off to a meeting one night and waited in the car until someone let me in. I wondered what other people thought of me, being the youngest person in the group, but the lesbians took me under their wings and I discovered that they were actually pretty cool.

The discussion that took place at the meeting covered a lot of topics, including adoption rights (or lack thereof at the time), and it really inspired me to get more involved in the issues that affected my community. I grew up in a political family and was active with the youth wing of the Liberal Party on both the provincial and national levels. In preparing for the 2002 biennial convention, the Young Liberals put forward a few policy resolutions and one of the ones that passed involved benefits for same-sex couples. That became a policy objective for the federal party and I was very proud to be a part of it.

That same year, I published a book of poetry with Jesperson Press called *The Teenage Years . . . Mapped*. The book had five chapters and each one focused on a different area of a teenager's life—finding love, losing love, family, identity and dealing with death for the first time. I didn't change the "he" pronoun when referring to love even though I was male. The idea of putting the book out with *that* in it was a bit nerve-wracking. But I got over it because it was about so much more than my sexuality. It focused on being a normal teenager, finding your way through all of the challenges, misunderstandings and feelings of isolation you face as you go through those years. Yes, defining sexuality was a part of it, but not the only part. To me, "gay" was "normal" (for lack of another word) and that part didn't need to be highlighted any more than the other parts of the book.

When I started university, I still felt strongly about helping my community. I found out about a resource centre called LBGT-MUN and decided to check it out. I circled the corridor, which was also known as "the fruit loop," a few times before entering, and the people there embraced me like family. Shortly after that, I ran for the position of General Director. By this time, NGALE had dissolved and Pride was fast approaching, so LBGT-MUN stepped up and made it happen that year. We also developed a guide for LBGT students and distributed copies all over campus. The best part about it, for me, was that my mom wrote about us in it. She wanted to share our story to let others know that the reaction isn't always bad and that she couldn't be more proud.

Josh exits.

MONOLOGUE 11

Young

Philip Goodridge

*We hear a faint sound of Cher's "Do you believe in life after love,"
as if coming from inside a bar. The setting: the alley behind a dance
club. Dance music is very faint in the background. Phil enters. He is
drunk. He is wearing an ill-fitting tank top and jeans. He is drenched
in sweat and his face is flushed from dancing. He holds a cigarette
and occasionally checks his iPhone. His tone is always upbeat, even
when speaking of negative things; he has reached a sort of state of
euphoria. Nothing can faze him.*

The tank top was a mistake, I realize that now. But it's too hot
in there anyway and my shirt is gone. Doesn't matter why.
Doesn't matter why. Do you have a light? (*A second club goer–not
visible– indicates he doesn't.*) I haven't had one of these in seven
years. I probably shouldn't, I'm not even craving it, you know,
I just want to.

I haven't been dancing in years . . . actual years, not like "oh
so long ago," like months ago—like actual years. Yeah, I'm here
by myself. I texted around to a bunch of my friends and they're
all, like, "Mmm, not really feelin' it," . . . "Naw, I'm too old for
that place now." Too old—what's too old? I don't remember an
age restriction. There's a guy in there who's 90 if he's a day! Yeah,
no, he is creepy, but that's not the point. I can't talk—if anyone of
them had asked me even last week to come out here I would've
said the same thing. (*Checking his phone, then checking back in.*)

Last time I was here this tank top actually fit me. I mean look
at this. This? (*Indicating belly.*) This isn't going anywhere. And I
totally don't even care. I totally do. Whatever. So I'm fat

and old. See?! See?! Right there!! And that's the problem! I'm only thirt…in my 30s! And I'm pretty healthy!! And I'm calling myself fat and old. What's gonna happen, 10 years and 2,000 tubs of cream cheese down the road? I don't just eat it with a spoon, I use it in stuff—that's not the point, the point is: people act like a gay man reaches old age at 28!! I feel like I should have a t-shirt that says "Be kind to seniors." Oh my God, I totally need a t-shirt that says "Be kind to seniors." I mean, you already feel old, don't you? (Sarcastic.) And you're like what, 5? No, that's mean.

You don't smoke? Someone out here must have a lighter. You know what's wrong with young people today? Nothing. Everything. I mean everything and nothing. I feel like when I was a kid everyone thought the Earth was doomed in our hands. You guys are doin' alright.

"You guys"—listen to me, calling you "you guys"—but you know what I mean, you guys are way ahead of the game. I came out when I was 15. I was known as "The Gay Kid." Well, I was actually "The Other Gay Kid"; there were two of us back then. And there was none of this happening. (Holding up his phone.) I found chat rooms—yes, CHAT ROOMS—when I was, like, 19. There was no "Hey, you lookin'" or "pics to trade" shit. Oh that reminds me, one sec… (He checks his phone.)

Ha. Gross. This? If this existed when I was a teenager? All hope would be lost. It would've been dirty . . . er. My slutty phase would have been a slutty onslaught. Heh heh heh, no, I will NOT be getting laid tonight. I could, but I won't. ANYBODY could, Jesus, don't enter into this too lightly. I mean look at how many people are on here! (Shows him his phone screen.) See, that's a pro to being old. Old-er—yes, yes, I know. But I missed this hookup revolution. Which is definitely for the best. Sort of.

And you know what else is great? Facebook didn't exist until I was 30!!! Thank JESUS! I don't know how you guys do it. Everyone's comin' out in junior high and, and posting every ridiculous thought they've ever had. I'm not saying you did, I'm saying that's what I would've done—Christ, I was a very emotional lad, the things I would've posted. God, the POETRY! Ugh! The melancholy, angsty, only-gay-in the-village prose riddled through Hillroy exercise books. Gone, lost forever, engulfed in flames. Thank God. And there is no photographic evidence online of my past douche-baggery. You be careful. Because pictures can be . . . incriminating . . .

Man I would never want to go back to that. But you seem to have your shit together. I mean, there's tons of you. The bar is filled with you. When I was 20, I knew five gay guys. Five. And they were all old enough to be my father. Oh my God. I'm actually old enough to be your father. Weird. *(Trying to smoke his cigarette.)*

This isn't even lit. And I can't believe you're wearing a Smashing Pumpkins t-shirt. *Siamese Dream* came out, like, 20 years ago. When I was your age, 20 years ago was THE '70S! Smashing Pumpkins, your t-shirt . . . you don't know who they are? Jesus Christ, take it off, take off your shirt—no, that came out wrong, please leave it on. But for God's sake do your research.

Your friends are staring. And it's not because I'm hot. *(He laughs.)* Seriously, mark my words, they'll be all like, "Why were you talking to that weird old guy?" HA! No, man, I'm having a wicked time. I'm not saying any of this to make you feel sorry for me. *Au contraire, mon frère.* Yes, I did just say that and I apologize. No, man, I feel . . . fantastic. This may just be the best day of my life. Honestly? It's my birthday. Yup . . . 35. *(Pause. Revelation.)*

You know what? I was actually gonna lie! See? I was gonna say, "Old enough" or "30ish" or "30 again this year"! Which is stupid! Why would I do that?! Ha ha ha. Why? Ha ha ha, because I'm insecure, that's why. Aaaaaah, look at me, I'm disgusting. NO! Ha ha ha ha, because I've been sweating like a whore, I'm flushed, and I've been rolling around in the dirt, ha ha ha ha! And that's the point isn't it? They say: dance like no one's watching, right? *(Pause.)*

Oh my God, your shoes cost more than my house. I'm not here to be seen. I'm here to have fun. You can forget that after a while. You worry about wrinkles and gettin' doughy but, whatever. More often than not, when you think all the guys are sitting there laughing at you and judging? They're probably not even paying attention to you. And sometimes they are laughing at you. But . . . why would you kill yourself to impress a bunch of arseholes? *(Looks at phone.)* Oh my God, look at this! Someone just posted this, like 10 minutes ago—it's me dancing on the speaker. I had no choice, it was Cher! *(Laughing.)* Ah, you don't understand. *(Still laughing.)* Oh GOD I look like a bloated mole rat. I'm making this my profile picture. That . . . that is special. *(Looking at cigarette.)* I'm not gonna smoke this. Do you want it? *(Hands the cigarette, takes it back.)* Good man. *(A song is audible, Rhianna.)*

Yeah, no, totally, you go back, it's Rhianna, I totally understand. God no, I can't go back in there, I think my lung exploded during the whole Cher debacle. I am going to go eat my weight in poutine, vomit, and pass out. Hopefully in that order. You, fine sir, go do embarrassing things and rejoice in them. And when you find your first grey hair, remember this night, and remember . . . grey hair is hot! HOT! *(Heading off.)* I am 35!! I am 35!! Smoking kills!!! *(He steps offstage and vomits.)*

Phil exits. Lights out. Black. Lights on. Curtain Call.

CPSIA information can be obtained at www.ICGtesting.com
Printed in the USA
LVOW05s1126100314

376507LV00004BB/7/P